# Each Moment We're Alive

## A Musical and Photographic Story
### Inspired by Cancer Survivors

by *Debra Lynn Alt*

Photographs by *Monica Schwartz Baer*

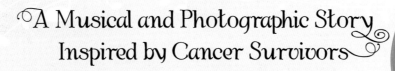

Music CD Included

Balboa Press books may be ordered through booksellers or by contacting:

Balboa Press
A Division of Hay House
1663 Liberty Drive
Bloomington, IN 47403
www.balboapress.com
1 (877) 407-4847

ISBN: 978-1-4525-1880-0 (hc)

Library of Congress Control Number: 2014919425

Print information available on the last page.

Balboa Press rev. date: 6/29/2015

BALBOA
PRESS
A DIVISION OF HAY HOUSE

To Monica, my Mom, my Dad, and all those whose cancer took away far too many precious moments of life.

# EACH MOMENT WE'RE ALIVE — THE MUSICAL AND PHOTOGRAPHIC STORY...

The story of how this book came to be, started with the friendship between Monica and myself in 2003. Two passionate Jewish women living on the shoreline of Connecticut, together we formed a sweet and unusual bond. The first time I heard about Monica was when I picked up my daughter Melody from Hebrew school in a mood strikingly brighter and more animated than the one she was in when I managed to drag her out of bed for her Sunday morning ritual. When I questioned my 11-year-old on her class, I discovered that her teacher Monica was not only a child of 2 holocaust survivors, but that she was also a breast cancer survivor. Clearly, the way this teacher was communicating her story was having a remarkable impact on my little student.

Not long after that Sunday morning, Melody announced that her teacher was retiring to follow her passion for wildlife photography. Although disappointed to learn we would be losing such an amazing teacher, my heart warmed at the idea of someone declaring that they were about to embark upon their lifelong dream journey of fulfillment. Fortunately the career change did not rule out private tutoring, so I arranged for Monica to tutor Melody privately for bat mitzvah lessons. Thus began our friendship, a bond forged largely over mutual care and concern for my daughter. Monica had an incisive ability to reach Mel in a way no one else seemed to touch.

At the time my Dad was being treated for acute leukemia, and Monica gave new meaning to empathy for what I was going through. During those last months of my father's life, the Misha Be'rach, the traditional Hebrew prayer of healing, was a difficult melody for me to sing or hear without crying, and Monica was always present to chant, hug, support. We became each other's soul sister, each championing the other in our respective artistic mediums, photography and songwriting.

As Chairperson for the American Cancer Society's Relay for Life Survivor Committee, Monica approached me one day to consider writing a song for the fifth anniversary of her town's relay for life event. Monica arranged for me to interview a group of survivors to base my song on and I wrote "Each Moment We're Alive". I then recorded it in Nashville along with the other songs I put on my second CD, In Broad Daylight, which was dedicated to my father. I performed it with a band at the North Branford Relay for Life in June of 2008, while the survivors swayed in the heat of that emotionally charged June day. We gave out copies of the song to the survivors and it was amplified while hundreds walked around the traditional track led by a proud flag-bearing Monica who had received citations from state officials earlier that day for her exemplary community service.

Monica was first diagnosed with Hodgkin's disease in 1981 at the age of 24. In 2003 breast cancer was found as a result of radiation treatment for the Hodgkin's. This survivor event marked the 5-year anniversary of not only her breast cancer diagnosis, but also the Relay for Life survivor committee. The following year, Monica was hit again with a diagnosis, this time metastatic stage 4 breast cancer to the bones. It was around this time that we started to think about the idea of collaborating on a book featuring Monica's photography as an illustration of our bond, and the desire to leave a legacy of our collective heart's desires. We set out to publish a book to help inspire others to pursue their dreams despite obstacles, to leave a legacy of enduring friendship art and passion. Each image is presented in light of how it reflects a moment of being alive. Together we hoped to share our collective spirit of aliveness in a book that celebrates the marriage of music and photography, of love and hope, of triumph over adversity, and all that brings light to the world.

We had to work quickly to publish as Monica's health and energy were dwindling. In the summer of 2012 we had events for our first soft cover edition of *Each Moment We're Alive*. The first was at Monica's home with family and friends, and I remember with great fondness the effort and pride she poured into inscribing each book. The other was a memorable well-attended event in June of 2012 at RJ Julia's in Madison, Connecticut. It was preceded by interviews with local publications and publicity for the iconic shoreline bookstore whose reputation for sponsoring authors was highly thought of. Wheelchair assisted, it was Monica's last outing. She spoke, signed as many books as she could, and I performed the song with my friend and songwriting partner, Jeff Fuller. It was a gift for all present, and especially wonderful for my dear friend Monica.

Although this has become my project to carry on, I am moved by the memory of a friend with whom I shared the deepest connection imaginable. Toward the end of her life, we talked of how we believed that the concentration camp scars that her parents carried were passed onto the next generation emotionally and perhaps even biochemically. Art was the only way we could fathom to harbor hope that the world could heal the insurmountable wounds of that dark time in history. The song and the photographs are offered as a tapestry for a world we refused to surrender to total darkness.

The development of electronic media has eclipsed many traditional art forms, from cursive writing to the book you are reading. *Each Moment We're Alive* fulfills my promise to make this book widely available and expresses the value of beholding beauty in our hands to treasure and share. This gift edition includes my latest CD compilation of songs recorded in Nashville. Going back to the studio to rerecord the song for this edition gave me an opportunity to create new versions of other meaningful songs including those I've written for other causes. I wanted to archive these songs with a clear and fresh contemporary sound with the best possible musical production. I've included my song for Habitat for Humanity, M.A.D.D. (Mothers Against Drunk Driving), child abuse, and autism. There is also one written on the occasion of my parents' 50th anniversary, one written for my home state of Connecticut, and a new love story. The CD ends on a sacred note with a healing prayer heard in congregations throughout the world.

The suffering and intensity of the cancer journey is so personal that it's impossible to explain in words alone. I hope these songs and pictures will be a canvas for communicating, sharing and expressing the universal experience for survivors and caretakers alike.

Captions under the photos are Monica's personal reflections of her experience of capturing each one, as she explained them to me.

*Debra Lynn Alt, June 1, 2015*

Please don't offer sympathy
It's hard for me to hear
how you feel sorry

**Seeing Eye to Eye**

Walking through the rhinoceros section of the Lion Country Safari in Florida, I noticed many magnificent birds visiting the habitat. Catching an ibus staring directly at the rhino was a remarkable display of harmony amongst God's resplendent creatures. The disparity evokes thoughts of how wonderful it would be if humans could create harmony, despite the vast differences between us.

Some say we're closer to a cure each day

But still my body turns away to betray me

## Three Monks

At Niagara Falls I noticed a band of orange lit by sunlight and I watched three robed men take in the splendor of the Falls. As I wondered about their thoughts and life experience, I found myself in awe of their presence and felt it was a moment well worth distilling.

What I really want is for you to know

you to know

Just what it is when my

story's told

That sustains me

**Jordan Pond in Fog**
The first light of early morning holds not only a precious energy, but illumination of the most beautiful kind. At Acadia National Park in Maine, with about 30 others attending a seminar led by a notable wildlife photographer, I was drawn to the contrast of the fog and red rocks and I longed to compose this gorgeous drama. A personal favorite of my husband's.

It's a strength that somehow
makes its way

Through all the words and
the simple faith

That I'll make it

**Dinner Delivery**

I fell in love with an osprey nest in Madison, Connecticut. Literally spending hours watching the birds fly in with fish they dug out of the river to bring to their babies, for several days in a row I watched patiently behind the reeds. Day after day I crouched, surrounded by mosquitoes and a nearby port-a-potty, until the day when I caught the delivery of a headless fish to the 4 young offspring. After all that time I had begun to feel connected to this family and was truly excited to catch the moment. With my remote shutter release and intense focus on the nest, I captured the moment of triumph with deep excitement and a feeling of having fulfilled my dream of becoming a wildlife photographer.

I say, cancer cannot cripple love

Or shatter hope

Or be anything

But angry

**Maid of Mist**
Taken from the American side of Niagara Falls, watching a boat navigate through the angry rushing waters.

W hen you work so hard

to stay alive

You need a reason pushing

you to strive

To keep going

**Hummingbird**

Catching this bird mid-flight was thrilling in so many ways. I put much time and effort into making it conducive for the bird to stay for a while in my backyard. I arranged flowers in such a way to be able to catch her at the right moment. I must have taken 300-400 pictures that day to ensure that I would be able to see her tongue reach toward the flower, as well as the details of the wings as they propelled the hummingbird at her amazing speed. Total exposure of a moment as sweet as the nectar that brought her to me.

It's a message
It's a wakeup call

**Hands Up**

Strolling through Bandelier National Monument in Los Alamos, New Mexico, two friends and I relished the sweetness of sharing. We discussed our personal coping strategies and in a lighthearted moment the idea of putting up your hands to shift energy is suggested and exemplified. Framed with trees as an archway, I wanted to capture the spontaneity that came from our camaraderie that fine day.

It's a plea to understand it all
And find meaning

## Generations

Attending a native American pow-pow called Schemitzun in Uncasville, Connecticut was truly awe inspiring. The participants were in full costumed regalia which spoke beautifully of the color and passion of their tribal unity. After the main dance ended, one of the leaders still glistening from the sweat of his exuberant moves, stopped at the side of the stage and spontaneously lifted his infant son from his stroller. How sweet to catch a moment of pure expression and reverence for the fruit of his familial blessings.

For the scary roller coaster ride

**Flying Wallenda**

At the North Haven Fair in Connecticut in the summer of 2011, with the setting sun as a backdrop. I watched as a 14-year-old performed her daring stunt silhouetted against the sky. It captured for me that "Go for it all, take risks while embracing life" attitude with stunning beauty.

And the hope

That never leaves my side

For long

**Good Morning Key West**
On my way to the pier in Key West, Florida, I watched the sun gradually rise and peak through the clouds early one morning. Nearby birds gathered for a compositionally perfect moment of silhouette against the sky.

# In each moment we're alive

**Mr. Murray**
Named playfully by my daughter, we watched this delightful primate for quite a while, devouring his quirky personality. It made me so happy to watch his facial expressions shift and I wanted to show what I thought were the more smile-eliciting moments.

# With every chance we let slip by

**Winter in Vermont**

One Vermont winter I was surprised to pass by a frozen lake where upon their lounge chairs, two guys created a rare scene. I adore the quirky sweetness of this image.

There's something to remind us
why we're here

**Bar Harbor Leaves**

In my first official photo contest where I was competing against those who at the time were far more accomplished and equipped than I, I competed for a first place prize of a Nikon Coolpix camera. Walking around the hotel, I caught the water formation on turning leaves from the sprinkler system. More than just the luscious simplicity of this photo, this one was a sweet affirmation of my early and eager passionate ambition.

# In each moment we're alive

**View from Mount Greylock**

On one of my many foliage trips, one night I headed to the top of this mountain to see the sunset. Cropped for a panoramic feel, I found the magnificent lighting and colors to be sensational and a breathtakingly beautiful image that I felt successfully reflected what I saw.

In what it takes to have survived

**Sturdy Shelter**

Sometimes an appealing moment of natural composition evokes a likeable concept. By a small lake outside a butterfly sanctuary in southern Florida, I was taken by this cormorant seated on a duck decoy. I found myself imagining a friendship and mutual dependency between this large seabird and inanimate wooden creature. I longed to capture this quirky idea.

# The beauty of our presence is so clear

**Birdwing**

How delightful to capture the iridescent colored butterfly sucking nectar out of a flower. Taken at Butterfly World in southern Florida.

# I'm counting off my milestones

## A Shoe-In

When I heard that a certain Alaskan politician was scheduled to speak at the Autism Walkathon in Westchester, New York where Deb was scheduled to sing, I felt the biggest photo op inspirational pull. Without divulging my political inclinations, let's just say I had to see this character in person for myself. The image I chose to share with the world is that moment when she transformed from her on-stage red shoes to her sneakers. I felt that those of us still trying to wrap our brains around this woman's presence would appreciate this moment.

And count on friends
and loved ones to

stick by me

**Family Portrait**

What a treat to see an intimate ape family scene while visiting the Edinburgh Zoo in Scotland. I couldn't take my eyes off of them. How fascinating to observe their family hierarchy, their expressions of affection and maternal protectiveness. I found this honest display of family interaction fascinating and very beautiful.

# I'll keep holding onto miracles

**Solitude**

Prescott Park is one of many beautiful parks in the area of Portsmouth, New Hampshire, and I was drawn to the way this tree evoked a desire to be embraced by the wisdom its shelter seemed to promise. I wanted to connect with the tree and believed that it offered a spot that beckoned me to sort out some thoughts and feelings not typically accessible.

Or better still

The strength of will

To beat this

## Miss Martha

In a Mexican restaurant in Miami I witnessed a 90th birthday celebration, complete with songs and hats and much reverie. What was most remarkable to me was the way the family revered this woman. Dressed to the nines in a meticulous white linen jacket, her face belied much character, class, elegance and wisdom. I introduced myself and soon Martha and I went to a quiet spot away from her rambunctious family where she honored me with her time and this photograph.

I can't believe

I went through all this pain

To say that it's been all in vain

**War and Innocence**

Particularly proud of this, a shot a photography teacher coined a one-in-a-million. I had heard about a church in Connecticut where locals had placed an American flag on the lawn for each soldier who died in Iraq. As I observed a family taking it in, I asked if I could photograph the back of a young girl facing this powerful vision.

# It's changed me

**Jumping on Arthur's Seat**

There is a unique joy one has when you witness your child's genuine happiness. My daughter fell in love with Scotland when she studied abroad there. When I came to visit her, we climbed up to Arthur's Seat, a main peak in Edinburgh, to view this clear and magnificent spot. In this moment I wanted to capture her enchantment with this gorgeous country.

# N ow I spread the word of what I know

## Curb Appeal

The relative barrenness of long stretches of highway near Phoenix Arizona began to look like an empty palette. I noticed a sudden splash of color on the side of the road that begged for me to turn around to examine further. After driving several miles in both directions, I got back to the spot and delighted in the color and liveliness of this fabulous off-road view.

And what it means to take it slow

And be grateful

**Key West Sunset**
I discovered a Key West town with a lovely tradition of celebrating each sunset at the beach, honoring the particularly consistent perfection of this geographical location. Mesmerized by the huge boats sailing into the proverbial sunset, I waited for just the right one to pass. This moment evokes for me a longing to be a passenger on a ship leading to nowhere. I love its magnificence against the orange sky.

# For each moment we're alive

**A Touch of Pink**

At the Bridge of Flowers in Shelburne Falls, Massachusetts, this breathtaking scene caught my eye. I loved the background of reeds that looked like blades of grass offset by the flower popping out from the leaves. The imperfect beauty of it all filled me with joy.

For every breath,
With every sigh

**Snuggle Time**

I love primates and have spent much time at the Bronx Zoo watching them. At the Congo exhibit I found myself focusing on this mother nurturing her baby for a long time. Deeply drawn to the attention and affection given by this mom, I found them in the corner through glass and a long lens. A multi-award winning shot, it warms my heart and always brings a smile to my face as it evokes thoughts of snuggling with my own child.

# How the world will be so different from now on

**Rue Abesses**

A moment captured in the Montmartre section of Paris. I waited a long time for this shot, calling upon much patience on top of this famous street until the perfect fashionable Parisian came along to help me paint the picture.

# In each moment we're alive

**Rustle**

Had to include my precious baby boy whom we adopted from a shelter after he came over to me and sat in my lap, affectionately noting he did not try to rustle away from me, as did most other kittens.

I want to fill my heart's desire

**Just Married**
This image was one I literally followed a crowd to capture. Having just left the Basilique Notre-Dame De Montreal, we saw crowds following a couple that had just left their wedding ceremony. I saw a sweet opportunity and acted as if I was one of the local photographers for the event. Seems like that 'just married' moment is one that many are drawn to. So on the street outside the church, the new bride and groom put on a show to satisfy the romantic onlookers.

Toss caution to the wind
And reach beyond

**Eilean Donan Castle**
Right before the Isle of Skye in Scotland, sits this breathtaking castle caught with a dramatic sky, setting the stage for the magnificence of the country and the immensity of its beauty.

In each moment we're alive

We follow joy

We carry pride

**True Love Never Grows Old**

On a Boston street where I would go to visit my daughter in college, I often noticed a particular couple walk by, always holding hands. On this day I was struck by their similar clothing, walking in step, seemingly so connected to each other. I captured this endearing couple's step in time.

# Empowered to be all we're Meant to be

**Portland Headlight**

I've often traveled to Maine in the summertime, but I decided I wanted to experience its stark beauty mid-winter. I had heard there was a beautiful lighthouse located off the beaten track and I was determined to capture it in the splendor of first morning's light. In order to do so I had to wake up in temperatures below 4°F. Bundled up at 6am, I drove 30 minutes from where I was staying, climbed over cumbersome wire fencing with my camera equipment, and framed what looked to be the quintessential New England lighthouse. I am immensely proud of my frigid Maine morning's photo.

# In each moment we're alive

**New Hampshire Horse Farm**

Sometimes creating a beautiful photograph requires taking chances. I spotted a lovely farm while driving in New Hampshire. I pulled over and asked this sketchy-looking guy if I could venture more deeply into the property even as I had my doubts as to the safety of doing so. I felt that the willingness to face my fear helped create the magic of this scene.

# From everything that can inspire

**Ambelside Sunset**

One perfect day while rambling through the lake district of England, I caught this moment on a small dock in a beautiful town. A quintessential picture perfect moment with a life affirming scene of father and child literally in the glow of the sun setting.

# Entrust that life will give us what we need

**Silhouette**
At the Bronx Zoo aviary, catching the sweet precision of one bird feeding the other. I love the starkness of the image, with its almost fine-art element.

# In each moment we're alive

**Tree of Light**
How fitting that my last photo of the book was taken at the last vacation spot I came to for a gallery showing my work, before we went to print. At the Seaport Village in San Diego I was drawn to these amazing trees with incredibly smooth bark that I found evoked power in their barrenness. I felt it was meant to be that I would find the sun through the hole in the bark as a ray of hope, evoking a high presence and the deepest sense of "besheret".

## DEBRA LYNN ALT

Debra Lynn Alt is a singer-songwriter originally from New York City. She has performed in venues throughout the New York metropolitan area and has been in musical theater, and country, rock and club date bands, most notably the Rolling Stone Magazine house band in 1979. She moved with her daughter to the shoreline of Connecticut in 1999 where she produced three CDs of mostly original songs entitled "A Spirited Mother", "In Broad Daylight", and the CD enclosed in this book. Her interest in incorporating philanthropic work with her music began when she wrote a song for a child abuse agency that her parents were helping with, and donated proceeds from her CD to that organization. Since then she has performed at various benefits and volunteered as a singer at the Connecticut Hospice for events and bedside comfort. She continues with her effort to write songs to raise consciousness as well as funds for causes. In addition to "Each Moment", she has written songs for autism, the MADD Song (for Mothers Against Drunk Driving), and Habitat for Humanity. Debra accompanies herself on piano and guitar and continues to perform at special events, and write and record. Her music has been referred to as "cause and just-because music".

www.debralynnalt.com

## MONICA SCHWARTZ BAER

Monica Baer's career began as a Hebrew and religious school teacher. In 2005, she took a transforming trip to Montana that left her with a deep sense of peace and purpose for pursuing wildlife photography. She was accepted into Moose Peterson's "Master of Light Program" in September 2005 when she learned to channel her passion and humor into vivid unforgettable images. Her studies continued into digital photography usage and she has since shown and exhibited and sold her work at various art shows throughout Connecticut. She competed and received ribbons from numerous photography expos, including NECCC competitions. Two of her wildlife images hung in the Ordover Gallery housed at the San Diego Museum of Natural History at a special exhibit from January through May 2012. She resided in North Branford, Connecticut for 15 years. While she battled stage 4 breast cancer with metastasis to her bones, she worked hard at making the most of each precious moment. She passed away in the embrace of her husband Ken and daughter Lindsay on July 12, 2012.

## ACKNOWLEDGEMENTS

We wish to acknowledge those people that have encouraged and supported the publication of this book. Our respective husbands and daughters, Ken, Steve, Lindsay, Melody, who helped us mostly by loving us unconditionally. By inspiring us to leave the ultimate legacy that is the timelessness of art, ensuring we will live on through the labor of so much love. Special thanks to Moose Peterson, world-renowned wildlife photographer (who recognized and encouraged Monica's talent). Much gratitude to the survivors, especially the ones that gathered to tell their stories that helped birth the song. Our friend Irene who helped us pull it all together, we're so grateful for your patience and talent. To our friend and co-writer Jeff Fuller for the music that helped carry "Each Moment". To Melissa, for your caring of the body and spirit beyond what one can conceive of a friend being able to deliver. With love to our respective fathers who instilled in us a desire to work hard, love generously and live each moment to the fullest. We relish your pride in what we've accomplished…… *Monya and Deb*

With special thanks to Dr. Wayne Dyer, Nancy Levin and those at the Hay House/Balboa Press Family that have inspired, recognized, and acknowledged the beauty of this project. And to all those who have worked with me and continue to carry the vision – Lori Diamond, Lisa Saunders and the Nice Girls, Sandra Wheeler, Kent Fuller, Jim Carpenter, John Mock, Sylvia Hutton, the Hurricanes at Super 9 Studios (Sandy & Irene), Ann Chadderton at Absolute Video, and all the other friends I cherish who live in my heart … with love and light always, Deb

**Back cover from left to right:**
Monica Schwartz Baer and Debra Lynn Alt in Deb's living room
*November 2010, photo by Steve Lazrove*

# EACH MOMENT WE'RE ALIVE

*Lyrics by Debra L. Alt, Music by Debra L. Alt & Jeff Fuller © 2008 Debra L. Alt & Jeff Fuller (ASCAP/BMI)*
*(DebraSong Music (ASCAP)/ Quadrangle Music (BMI)*

Please don't offer sympathy, it's hard for me to hear how you feel sorry
Some say we're closer to a cure each day, but still my body turns away to betray me
What I really want is for you to know just what it is when my story's told that sustains me
It's a strength that somehow makes its way, through all the words and the simple faith that I'll make it

I say cancer cannot cripple love or shatter hope or be anything but angry
When you work so hard to stay alive you need a reason pushing you to strive to keep going
It's a message, it's a wakeup call, It's a plea to understand it all and find meaning
For the scary roller coaster ride, and the hope that never leaves my side for long

In each moment we're alive, with every chance we let slip by
There's something to remind us why we're here
In each moment we're alive, in what it takes to have survived
The beauty of our presence is so clear

I'm counting off my milestones and count on friends and loved ones to stick by me
I'll keep holding on to miracles or better still the strength of will to beat this
I can't believe I went through all this pain to say that it's been all in vain, it's changed me
Now I spread the word of what I know, what it means to take it slow and be grateful

For each moment we're alive, for every breath, with every sigh
How the world will be so different from now on
In each moment we're alive, I want to fill my heart's desire
Toss caution to the wind and reach beyond
In each moment we're alive, we follow joy, we carry pride
Empowered to be all we're meant to be
In each moment we're alive, from everything that can inspire
Entrust that life will give us what we need
In each moment we're alive.........!

For music credits and production photos, see
music tab on website debralynnalt.com.